No Tongues To Speak

poems

Joseph Hart

ISBN: 978-81-8253-978-5

First Edition: 2022
Rs. 200/-

Cyberwit.net
HIG 45 Kaushambi Kunj, Kalindipuram
Allahabad - 211011 (U.P.) India
http://www.cyberwit.net
Tel: +(91) 9415091004
E-mail: info@cyberwit.net

for George Lane

Antithesis

Where rivers smoothest run
Deep are the fords.
The dial stirs,
Yet none perceives it move.
The firmest faith
Is in the fewest words.
Turtles cannot sing,
And yet they love.
True hearts have eyes and ears,
No tongues to speak.
They hear and see and sigh,
And then they break.

- Byron

"I like your Christ. I don't like your Christians."

- Gandhi

"Va pensiero..."

- Verdi

Contents

Dreams

Thinking of the world
With childlike understanding,
He sat upon the shore
And watched the seagulls landing.

Believing without reason
That there will be a dawn,
The gentleman is ruined,
But his mistress carries on.

A denizen of night
Where the dreams commence;
He meant everything he said,
And none of it made sense.

Lines

Chopin, Rachmaninoff,
Keats – all these -
And Ashkenazy at the keys -
Are beautiful things
And yet they die.
Can I forget this?
Should I try?

Or resurrect them
From the sea
And put their ghosts
Into poetry -

The Presidential Medal of Honor

Obama gave Perlman
The Medal of Honor -
A genius who plays violin.
Trump gave the medal to Limbaugh -
A bigot who liked him.

Lines

A trillion billion people!
Are all of them in heaven?
Egyptian, Aztec, Greek!
And where is God?

He's busily killing the kind.
Will the evil be triumphant?
Do mutated bones prove evolution?
Or Gods because
Someone imagined them?

Lines

Amazing that this bigot
With a swagger and a gun
Was once a little child who never
Hated anyone -

Poetry

Should a song be pretty?
Attempt to be profound?
Confessions of the soul?
An exercise in sound?

Sweet imagination?
Plain reality?
Convictions and beliefs?
What is poetry?

It's different in music,
With no purpose to declare;
The prosody of melody
Is already there.

The Stone

When I was a boy,
I found a colored stone,
Pretty, multicolored,
On the windowsill.
I picked it up and thought,
"If I hold this stone,
I will go insane.
But I'd only have
To come back again."
So I put it down,
And left it on the sill.

Keats & Millay

Pretty poems by Millay
I'm holding in my hand -
Only one or two of them
I cannot understand.

Ah but Keats! My precious Keats!
I've loved him since my youth.
Truth is rarely beautiful,
And beauty seldom truth.

The Meddlers

Parents of transgender children are being charged with child abuse, and their children are being taken away from them.

These superstitious meddlers
With their values and their morals
Want to oversee the lives of other people.
Who they injure doesn't matter
To their calling and their mission.
They won't stop. They won't stop.
Can't anybody stop them?

Lines

Such terrible pain!
Like the hope of the dying.
Don't look when he laughs,
And it sounds like he's crying.

Why?

So many decent people -
Scientists, composers -
Blown apart by bigots
With convictions and beliefs -
Following their madness
To the finish of us all -

Poems

Very special poems
By very special people -
With magic – such as Keats -
To read and read again -

Images and phrases
Like treasures from the sea -
Dredged up by a sailor
Who's a poet with a net -

Beauty! What is beauty?
Like Jesus, an illusion -
Are there special words
That indicate the soul?

An Ugly Poem

"Will they blow up the world today?
Tell me, mother, do."
Notwithstanding his conceit,
If he hadn't been a genius,
Keats would be forgotten too.
Disinterred, a corpse decays in heat.

In Oakland

I was sitting in a coffee shop
Smoking cigarettes
With a cup of coffee.
Two therapists came in.
I don't know how they knew
Where I was or when I'd be there.
They telephoned the cops
Who came and with a smile
Said, "We heard you're suicidal
And we want to help."
The cops took me away.
They drove me to a mental ward
And told me to get out,
Go anywhere I liked;
And then they drove away.
Maybe if I'd asked -
So very long ago -
I take my medication -
Can the madness come again?

"Is that all there is?"

All his life he worked.
He forgot about his youth.
He just continued working
Until he owned a house;
Then worked some more
Until he owned another.
Still he didn't stop
Or pause. And with two jobs
He kept acquiring houses.
Then when he was old,
Standing on the porch
He flipped his cigarette
On the perfect lawn,
Manicured and green -
As if he wondered
What he'd done it for.

Chaos

"Guernica"! Christ! What can anyone do?
Think of solutions. Get out of the fire.
Madmen make nonsense of all that you knew
Was probable, right. Even God is for hire.

Science reveals that the earth is a freak.
Lovable babies, endearing and new,
Grow up to be bigots. And each time you speak,
A man with a purpose shoots bullets at you.

The people you love are as foreign to you
As sailors and Chinamen over the sea;
Strangers. You talk to them. Each time you do,
You're holding a riddle, slippery, free.

You have no effect. And it's useless to try.
Nothing's as sure as the love of a cat.
Life is a promise. You're starting to cry
In futility. Nothing's as futile as that.

The Stray Cat

Sweet little cat
Alone in the wilderness
Running away -
Where is love?

Dinosaurs

She made a mockery of wisdom.
I have none.
Did a virus and a freeze
Kill the dinosaurs?
With nothing left but bones
Of the titans of the earth.
Will a virus and the heat
Kill the human race?
What about the animals?
They love.

Ukraine

Good men, decent men
Fighting in Ukraine -
Putting out the fires,
Dragging people from the wreckage -
With Russia telling lies
To justify its savagery -
Which can't be justified -

Lines

I've lost the battle.
It's pointless to fight it.
I've nothing to write
And no reason to write it.

Millay kept writing -
Page after page.
Keats stopped – but he died
At a very young age.

Housman wrote some
But not many books.
Poe even fewer.
Sadly it looks

Like I've lost any talent
I may ever have had.
Prolific! But cold
And prosaic and bad.

Lines

Like playing dice for the robes of Christ!
This is how it seems
To publish songs about the loss
Of the sweetest of my dreams.

MAGA

"Make America Great Again" -
Backwards we shall go
To the days of Joe McCarthy,
The evil of Jim Crow,
Keeping gays in closets
And women's status low -

Lines

(after hearing Mozart called "a dusty historic relic")

Mozart is a "relic",
His music only sound.
Philistines and God
Make the world go round.

Easily defeated,
Art was never strong -
A flower or a picture
Or a song.

The Past

Let me go back
To a beautiful time -
A time when art was gold -
Music was sweet,
Painting and books -
Why was beauty sold
To the lowest bidder?

Artists just in name -
Fame – without a reason -
Only fame -

Can I say what verse is?
Keats said "beauty". Poe
Said "rhythmed beauty". That
Is all I know.

Lines Without Rhythm

To leave my cats and treasures -
That's what it means to die.
The people in Ukraine
Are being murdered.
I don't know why.
Sartre and Camus
Dismissed heavenly love
In 1942.
Throughout all history
And before -
Art and Gods and war.

Lines

Music, books and pictures -
These are what I love.
My life was wasted
Following a star,
Away from these;
A rainbow;
There wasn't any gold.

Baudelaire, Rimbaud

Sweet relief from the English -
The only verse I know -
Neglected like an aging aunt -
Baudelaire, Rimbaud -
Phrases deep like spells -
How deep can phrases go?
Beautiful! Beautiful!
Sunlight on the snow -

Ukraine

The Ukrainians are dying -
How many of them poets?
Mothers with their children?
Children with their dogs?
They're praying to their Gods,
But only Putin answers.

For Dory Previn

The rhesus monkey and the cloth mother -
The boy and his teddy bear -
The paper describing Jesus
Tossed into the garbage by mistake
So there is no Jesus anywhere or ever -
Is heaven true
Or do I just want it to be?

John & Mary,

John and Mary – both of them are gone,
Long ago. Though time continues on,
And like an ocean wave across the shore,
Erases – quoth the Raven, “Nevermore” -

I cannot keep the thought of them at bay -
Or like a wizard, wave them both away.
Like the soft forgetting of the sea,
I’m waiting for the hour I can say,
“The sting is gone. It’s just a memory.”

The Good Men

Christians – are they Christian? -
This nonsense is unreal!
Holy men – other Gods forsworn -
Care more for a fetus
Before it starts to feel
Than they do
For those already born;
And masked and in the darkness
So no one can tell
Who they are burn crosses
That they think
Are saving them from hell.

My Last Duchess

There she sits. She's dead, you know.
Silent as a tomb.
We together pass our days
In this empty room.

She doesn't smile. She doesn't speak.
She doesn't walk or laugh.
That's what I want. My love song
Is an epitaph.

A marble sleep, shut eyes of wax;
I shall not marry thrice.
I murdered her. I did. Because
She was very nice.

The Magic Cat

When he was sick,
A cat came to his door
And slept upon his bed
From 4 til 4.

For many days, no months,
That cat stayed there,
A thing to pet and love,
The soul of care.

After he was well,
The cat lay on the floor,
Dead. He wasn't
Needed anymore.

Then he cried, "Come back
From heaven or from hell!
I love you, cat!
I never will be well!"

Freddy's Love

(a cat)

There was such a love
And happiness in Fred -
Just to be at home,
To love the hand that fed

His pink and tiny mouth.
Fred simply didn't know
In all his little world
Any way to show

His tiny heart's affection.
Who could understand?
So little Fred in love
Sprayed the person's hand.

The person was enraged
And with an angry shout
Picked up little Fred
And put him out.

Nightmare

He said he read minds.
Why would he lie?
There's an edge to the universe.
How and why?
Are there deities
In the sky?
Is there any reality
But music, love
And poetry?

Lines

Supremacists and bigots
Are on a killing spree.
ISIS is destroying
Archaeology.
Who is going to rescue you?
A shrink? A deity?
The damned of the abusive
Never will be free.
Preachers and composers
Die, the same as me.
Toss your stillborn baby
In the sea, the sea.

Lines, unfinished

Is afterlife a fantasy?
The deities a fact?
Suicide – and hopefully to go
To Elysium or heaven
While my mind is still intact -
All there is to know
Is Darin never burned
A heretic or witch -

Age

Animals stay beautiful
After they are old.
Then go away
And simply die alone.

People just get ugly –
Monsters of decay,
Unloveable -
Except by little children.

A Thought

I was sitting at a table
With my forearm on the surface;
And I saw the objects near me,
And I felt the things I saw.
The typewriter was blue
And with nausea and love
I saw it; and the table,
Square, impermeable, hard.
The flowers on the table,
In the living room, the sofa,
And the windows, and the edge of
The piano in the room
I saw, and felt in sensing.
In this consciousness, contentment;
And I heard the traffic passing
Out of doors, and it was evening
So as usual the cars
Seemed to make a sound of darkness.
Then I saw
A photograph of Keats
On the edge of the piano
And it was a hard sensation
Unresembling all the others;
In a sense, another thing.
For the photograph had meaning
That was personal to me.
And for a moment I believed that I

Would rather see the paper
That the photograph had come in,
Sent from London long ago.

(nominated for a Pushcart)

Lines

Look beneath his hoodie
On a winter night and find
The terrifying loneliness
Of a madman's mind.

The Poet

A tender ear for images,
An eye for perfect phrases,
He conjures up the alleys with his pen,
The destitute, the homeless,
The loveless and forlorn,
The sick, the sad, as though his words
Were savior to them all.
A broken mind embracing broken hearts,
He writes of the grotesques who have no skin,
But injured, wounded souls,
And that is all.

(nominated for a Pushcart)

The Wall

A fact that penetrated
The glass wall of my booth:
Tyrants hear what they want to hear;
They just don't hear the truth -

Values

After the ball is over
And they call out, “Change partners again!”
Do you sashay back to the first one,
And think of what might have been?

Are you old fashioned and dreamy,
Believing in Jesus, not luck,
Problems with only one answer,
And happiness more than a fuck?

That middle class love is what matters,
That madness and aging are lies,
Everyone’s basically decent,
And only a person cries?

The Misunderstanding

He brought flowers to the house,
Dried ones. I liked him.
I was uncomfortable, I said nothing.
I was afraid of saying something gauche.
Finally he said,
"I'll go find someone who wants to talk to me!"
And he left, and I was happy
Because it meant he'd wanted to talk to me.

Finish

Cast away love,
Science and God -
At 96 years
None of them matters -
And all that was good
Like music and art
Decays in a brain,
Becoming forgotten -

Lines

Eating meat is evil
But everybody does it.
That was God's intention.
I say – was it?

Their bigotry – their cruelty -
As if following a call
They invoke the name of God
To justify it all.

Lines

They love their little church
With Bibles and a steeple.
Trump brought out the worst
In almost half the people.

Why do they like Trump?
I never knew.
Another Jesus Christ -
And that makes two.

The Homecoming

1.

After many years wandering,
Wandering where
No deities answered,
He uttered no prayer.
He traveled and journeyed
On ocean and lands
Possessing no more
Than himself and his hands.
And then he came home.
He returned to them all.
He entered the castle
And stood in the hall.
His family welcomed him,
Each with a smile.
They bathed him and dressed him,
And each with a smile.
Healing the absence
That company mends,
The Saturday coming
They summoned his friends
For happiness, music,
Reunion and feast;
And for the occasion
They'd slaughter a beast.
The time trickled past
And the castle was dressed
In silver and curtains.

What joy it expressed!
"For you. For my son.
Now all partings are past.
My son," said his mother,
"Has come home at last."
And she smiled.

2.

He walked through the castle.
He wandered the halls.
He went to the sea
Where the swell-thunder falls.
He watched them prepare
For the upcoming feast.
He questioned his mother,
"Say, where is the beast
That we're going to eat
On that wonderful night
When we are together
And all becomes right?"
And she smiled.

3.

The days drifted by
And the party was near.
His mendicant heart
Felt the starting of fear.
The tables, the goblets,
The chairs and the plates

Were set and arranged
For this best of all fetes.
The draperies that
The old castle would wear
Were hung like a rose
In a prostitute's hair.
He nonetheless asked himself,
"What will we eat?
There are the apples,
But where is the meat"
He questioned the servants,
And each of them smiled.

4.

And then, then he knew,
Sardonic and grim,
What they would eat
At the feast would be him.
He ran to the doorway.
He rushed to the gate.
He fled down the road
To escape from the fete.
Then on the roadway
He suddenly paused.
He thought of the grief
Being human had caused.
He thought of the failures.
He thought of the fright.
He thought of the sweet
Celebration that night.
And he smiled.

5.

He turned on the causeway
And solemnly wept.
Back to the castle
His walking feet stepped.
There in the doorway
His mother had been
Waiting for him
To return once again.
And then when she saw him
She quietly smiled.
And reached to embrace him
And murmured, "My child."

6.

The party was gala.
The wine was supreme.
This verse was the sleep
That composes a dream.

Lines

I loved him forever.
He loved me a day.
Fetch up a casket
To take me away,
A heartless cadaver,
A corpse with no soul.
And off through the rain
Let the little cart roll
That carries my body
With nothing inside,
Gone like a wave
That goes out with the tide,
Over the cobblestones
Roughly I'll ride.
And no one will know
Or remember I died.
There on the bed
Of a small wooden cart,
Take my cadaver
That hasn't a heart,
Plod an old horse
Through the miserable rain,
Down to the graveyard
Where nothing feels pain.
I perished for love,
And I perished in vain,
Bones and a body,
And organs and brain,
But never a heart.

No, never again!
Deep, deep in a hole
Shall my body remain
'Til worms have devoured it.
I am insane.

The Statue

Carving at the statue -
Lines upon the face -
Marble legs and torso -
Carefully the hands -
Fingers made of stone -
Rough and grey and smooth -
Working after midnight
Lighted by the moon -
Working in the daylight -
Many many weeks -
Then finished with the statue -
Not another touch
Needed – he had better
Call his work complete.
He stopped and stared exhausted.
It couldn't be improved.
His single great achievement.
He lay beside the statue
And gently went to sleep,
And sleeping, slowly died.
A statue! As if God
Commissioned works of art!
As he rested dead,
The sky above grew darker,
Clouds amassed, black darkness
In the Heathen night.
A rain began to fall
On him beside the statue.
Then a shard of lightning
Shot out and struck the statue
And shattered it to dust.

The Friend

A felon in his cell -
A dark and concrete square -
Found a beetle crawling
In a corner.

With one extended finger,
Carefully he touched it.
The black and frightened beetle
Scuttled off.

The prisoner was happy.
His rough and dirty face
Smiled. He caught the beetle
In his hand.

He broke some twigs of straw
And put them in the corner.
He fed the beetle tiny
Bits of shit.

After several months
The crazy captive felt
The beetle was his friend.
He couldn't cry.

The warder on his rounds
Came into his cell,
Saw the bug and crushed it
With his boot.

A Tragedy

The farmer left his house
With a mallet and a gun.
"I'm going to kill that dog," he thought;
"And it will be fun."

The little boy just watched.
It was an easy kill.
He didn't do a thing,
And God was very still.

No one saw it happen.
He thought,"I wasn't brave.
I betrayed his trust.
And now he's in a grave."

The days continued on,
Though nothing lay ahead.
"I let him kill my dog,"
Was all he ever said.

JKD, another love song

Jay in Jersey. Not
The only friend I've had.
But one that I remember.
Not a thing was sad.

I met him in the library
In a quiet nook
Listening to love songs
While I read a book.

Totally uncritical,
Or else he did not see
Anything to criticize.
In happy irony,

He laughed, "You are a poet!"
What became of Jay?
He went back to India.
I just went away.

A winter passed in Hackensack,
Provincial little town.
He'd holler, "Fucking Hackensack!"
As the snow came down.

He was dark and pretty,
With hair as black as night.
I was only happy.
Everything was right.

Every day we'd visit
As evening drew near.
I would drink a soda.
He would drink a beer.

He said to get the forms
At the embassy
One needs to move to India.
I figured he meant me.

I pretended not to know
Why he wanted them. And he
In a rush of anger,
Threw them back at me.

He left me standing there -
Foolish in the rain.
He left. I left. And we
Never met again.

I've always had the fantasy
I saw him one time more -
Listening to records
As he'd done before.

Battle Hymn Of The Republic (after Julia Ward Howe)

Mine eyes have seen the glory of
The coming of the Lord.
If you have a couple billion
And you feel a little bored
America's a country you can
Easily afford.
The Truth is up to you.

In the beauty of the lilies Christ was
Born across the sea.
You can lock up little children.
You can alter history.
The supremacists will love you. You'll have
Immortality.
And God is on your side.

Oh! "You can grab a pussy."
Global warming isn't real.
Mexicans and immigrants
Are underneath your heel.
Like Jesus you'll be persecuted.
Animals don't feel.
When you are a star!

You'll feel mighty as an eagle with
Your woman standing there.
She will be an angel to all
Children blond and fair.
As for dark complected ones, she
"Really doesn't care."
Porn stars cost you dear!

Mock the weak, your fans will
Imitate the things you do.
Coin a phrase too infantile for
People over two.
Watch the children die and claim
It's not because of you.
You did nothing wrong.

The Christians call you holy. You're a
Saint among your kin.
You gave an extra meaning to
The noble thought of sin.
More popular than Jesus! You're
A little God of Tin.
A prophecy come true!

Standing like a Titan
And indifferent to tears,
A brain without an equal
And a penis with no peers;
Never mind the children.
You'll be President for years.
Iran don't frighten you.

The Constitution's history but
Meaningless today.
Science is ridiculous and
Reason is passe.
Bigots made you President and
They are here to stay.
God bless the USA!

Lines

I look in a mirror.
What do I see?
Can an ass
Write poetry?
Both the ass
And the poet are me.

Lines

One doctor said I'm "paranoid".
One wrote a book, and he
Said that paranoia
Is mediocrity.

So I haven't any talent
Or hope for poetry.
The least of all the art forms
Is too much for me.

www.ingramcontent.com/pod-product-compliance
Lightning Source LLC
Chambersburg PA
CBHW050024170726
48282CB00025B/540
* 9 7 8 8 1 8 2 5 3 9 7 8 5 *